WHAT IS SYMMETRY?

WHAT IS

Thomas Y. Crowell Company · New York

SYMMETRY?

By MINDEL and HARRY SITOMER
Illustrated by ED EMBERLEY

YOUNG MATH BOOKS

Edited by Dr. Max Beberman
Director of the Committee on School Mathematics Projects,
University of Illinois

Estimation
    by Charles F. Linn

Straight Lines, Parallel Lines, Perpendicular Lines
    by Mannis Charosh

Weighing and Balancing
    by Jane Jonas Srivastava

What Is Symmetry?
    by Mindel and Harry Sitomer

L.C. Card 70-101933

1 2 3 4 5 6 7 8 9 10

WHAT IS SYMMETRY?

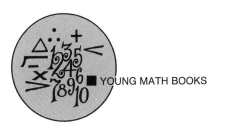

YOUNG MATH BOOKS

U.S. 1556354

Have you ever played the shake-shake game?

I put my right hand in.

I take my right hand out.

I give my right hand a shake, shake, shake,

And turn myself about.

I put my left hand in.

I take my left hand out.

I give my left hand a shake, shake, shake,

And turn myself about.

Your right hand matches your left hand.
Your right foot matches your left foot.
Your right shoulder matches your left shoulder.
Your head has a right eye and a left eye.
They match.
Your head has a right ear and a left ear.
They match.

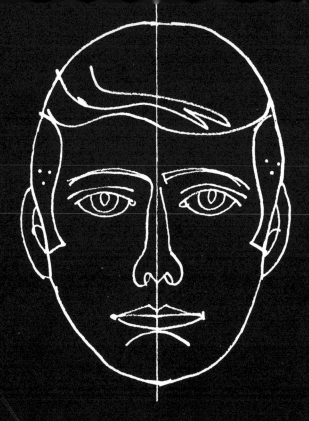

In this picture of a face there is a middle line. The eyes are balanced on each side of that middle line. The ears are balanced on each side of that middle line.

Is there a right nose and a left nose? Is there a right chin and a left chin? The nose and the chin are on that middle line.

The wings of a butterfly are balanced on each side of its body. They have the same size and shape. Sometimes, in flight, one wing fits exactly against the other.

This leaf is balanced on each side of its center rib. Each half of the leaf has the same size and shape as the other half.

This letter M is balanced on each side of the red line. Each half of the letter has the same shape and size as the other half.

This letter E is balanced on each side of the green line.

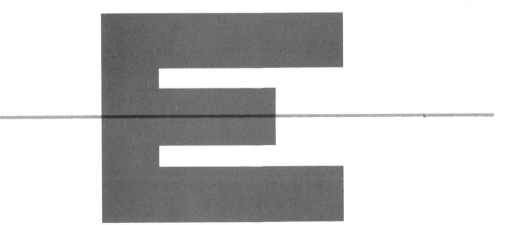

In the butterfly, the leaf, and the letters M and E, parts balance on each side of a middle line. The parts that balance have the same shape and size. This kind of balance has a name. It is called SYMMETRY. Because the parts balance on each side of a line, we call it LINE SYMMETRY.

You can find line symmetry in pictures of windows, doors, rugs, and curtain designs. Try to fold a picture along a line so that the parts on one side fit exactly over those on the other side. If there is a line like that, the picture has line symmetry. If there is not, the picture does not have line symmetry. We call this the FOLDING TEST for line symmetry.

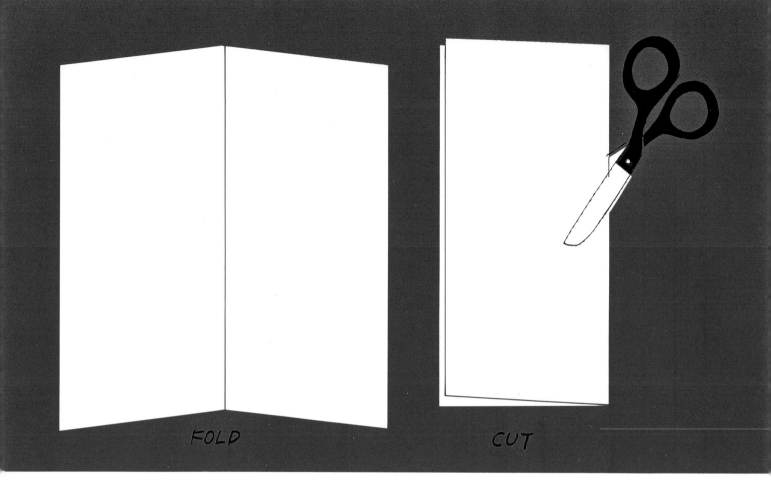

FOLD

CUT

You can use the idea of line symmetry to make designs. Fold a sheet of paper along the middle. When it is folded, cut out pieces—any shape you want, and as many as you want. Now open the paper flat. Do you see a design that has line symmetry?

UNFOLD

THE CREASE IS THE LINE OF SYMMETRY.

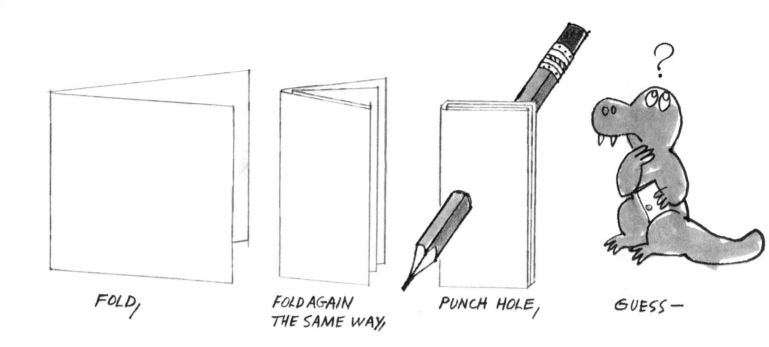

FOLD,

FOLD AGAIN
THE SAME WAY,

PUNCH HOLE,

GUESS —

Here is an experiment. Fold a sheet of paper in half. Then fold it in half again the same way. Punch a large hole through the four layers of paper, near the second crease. Before you unfold the paper, guess how many holes there are, and where they will be.

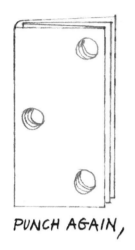

PUNCH AGAIN,

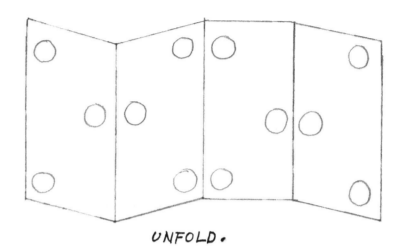

UNFOLD.

Now fold the same paper just as you did before. Punch two more holes near the other edge. Open the paper flat.

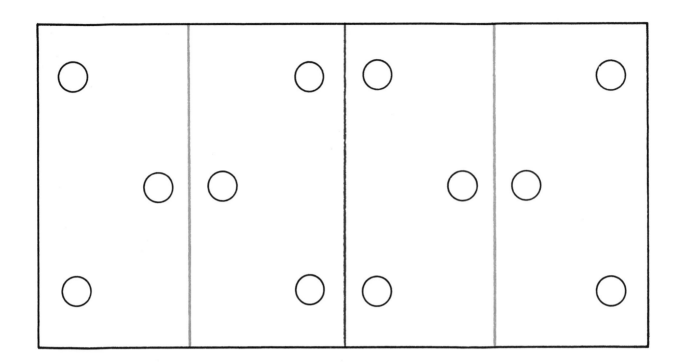

Color the crease in the middle red, and color the other two creases green.

It is easy to find line symmetries in the picture. Look at the red line. All six holes on one side of the red line match the six holes on the other side. Every hole is as far from the red line as the hole it matches on the other side. The twelve holes form a design that has line symmetry. Its line of symmetry is the red line.

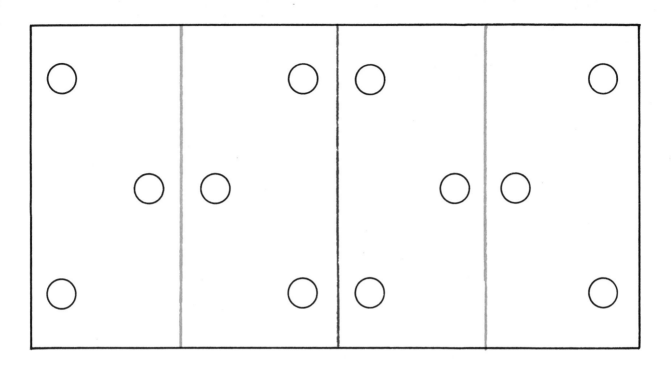

Now look at each of the green lines. Do the three holes on one side match three holes on the other side? If they do, then each group of six holes has line symmetry. The green line is the line of symmetry.

Fold a long piece of paper from top to bottom many times so that it looks like a fan or an accordion. Cut out paper dolls. Cut only on the dotted lines. When you open your paper, you have a string of dolls. Each doll has line symmetry, and the string of dolls also has line symmetry.

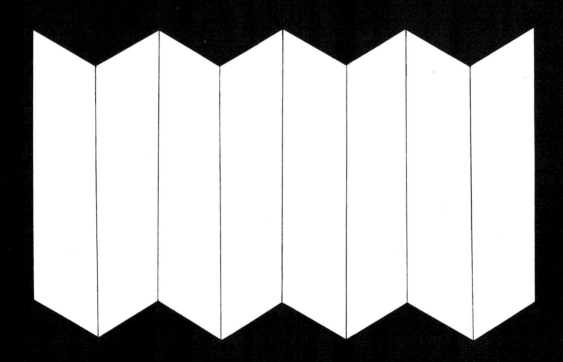

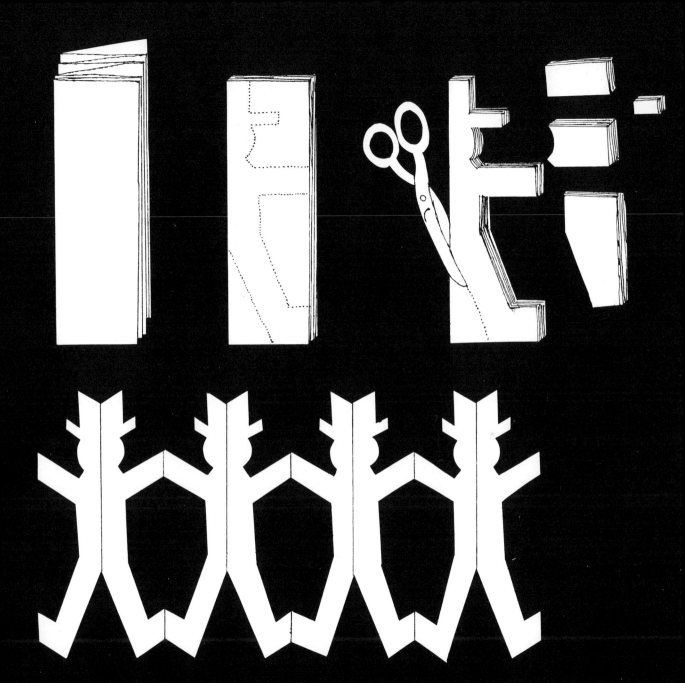

Line symmetry is important in science. Here is an example:

Two boys are playing with a ball. One throws the ball high in the air to the other. If you take pictures of the game with a movie camera, and then show the movie in slow motion, the path of the ball will look like this curve.

Imagine a fold along the red line. Would one part of the curve fit over the other? If so, the folding test works. The red line is the line of symmetry.

The paths of some comets are a lot like the path of the ball, but much, much longer. Scientists use symmetry to figure out these paths.

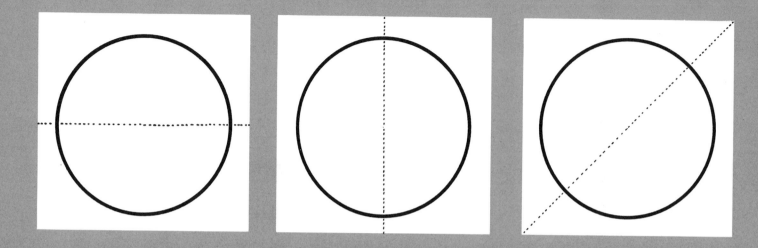

A circle has many lines of symmetry. You can easily see this if you imagine the picture of each of these circles folded along the dotted line.

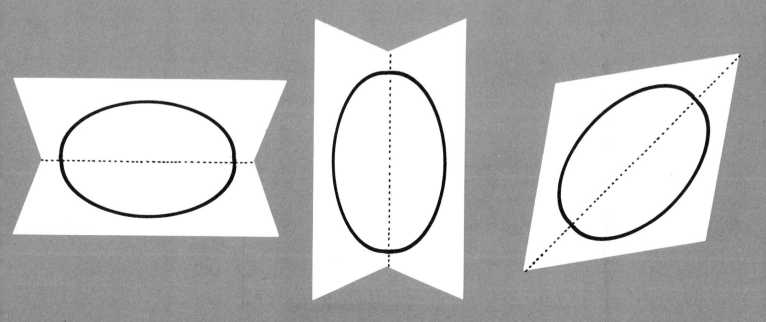

Have you seen a picture that shows the earth as it travels around the sun? The earth's path is called its orbit. It is not a circle. It is an ellipse. Copy the orbit on a sheet of paper. Can you fold this paper to show line symmetry? Can you find another way to fold it that shows line symmetry? The ellipse has two lines of symmetry.

This picture shows three flags and two lines. The lines make square corners at the black dot. Look at the red line. It is a line of symmetry for flags 1 and 2. The green line is a line of symmetry for flags 2 and 3. It looks as though flags 1 and 3 also balance. No matter how you try, you will not find a line of symmetry for flags 1 and 3—but these two flags do balance.

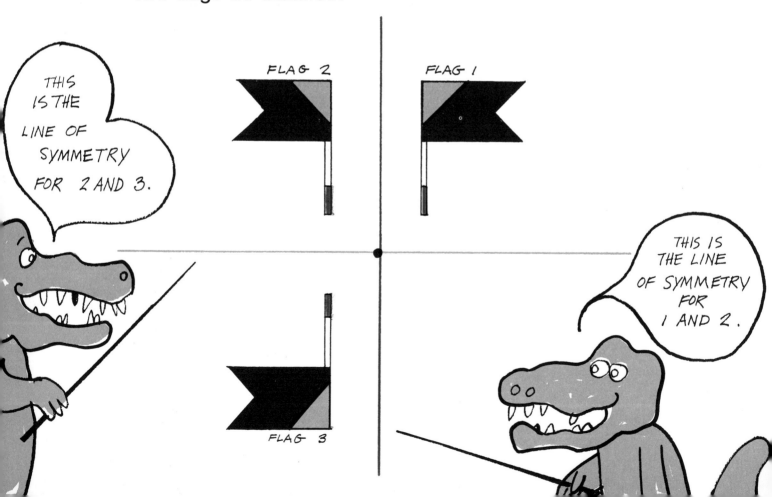

The green corners of the flags balance on each side of the black dot. The red ends of the flag-poles also balance on each side of the black dot. Every part of flag 1 balances a part of flag 3 on the other side of the black dot. This kind of balance is called POINT SYMMETRY, and the middle point is called the POINT OF SYMMETRY.

FLAG 1

FLAG 3

THIS IS THE POINT OF SYMMETRY FOR 1 AND 3.

This table, set for four people, has point symmetry. The black plates are balanced on each side of the black dot. So are the black forks and black spoons. The gray settings are also balanced on each side of the black dot. The black dot is the point of symmetry.

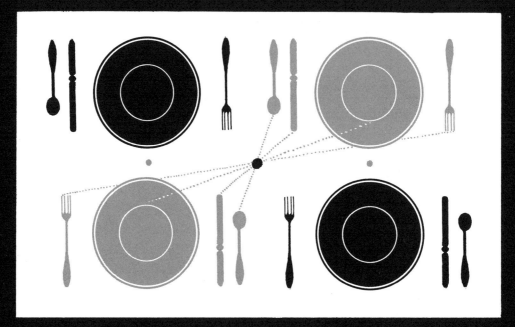

Look at the two settings at the right. Do you see that they have their own point symmetry? Where is the point of symmetry? Do you think that the two settings at the left also have their own point symmetry?

This design has point symmetry.

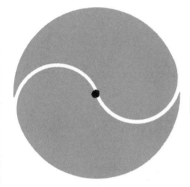

Here is the same design after it has been given a quarter-turn.

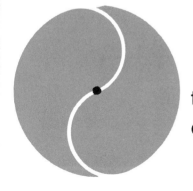

After a second quarter-turn in the same direction, or a half-turn altogether, it looks exactly as it did when we started.

Give the letter N a half-turn around the red dot.
Does it look the same after the half-turn? If it does,
then this letter N has point symmetry.

Is there a half-turn around any point in this three-leaf clover that leaves the picture looking the same? If there is no such point, then the three-leaf clover does not have point symmetry.

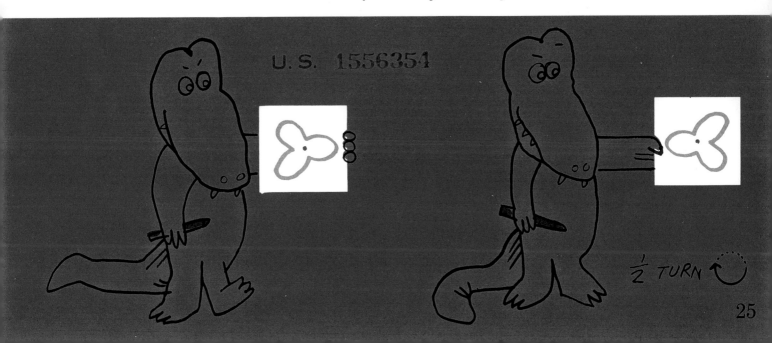

Here is an easy test for point symmetry:

If you can give a picture a half-turn around a point and not change the way the picture looks, then it has point symmetry. The point is the point of symmetry. If there is no such point, then the picture does not have point symmetry.

Draw a picture of a four-leaf clover that has point symmetry. Does your picture have line symmetry? Can you find four lines of symmetry?

This kite has one kind of symmetry but not the other. Which kind does it have? Which kind does it not have? Draw another kite that has two lines of symmetry. Does your drawing have point symmetry?

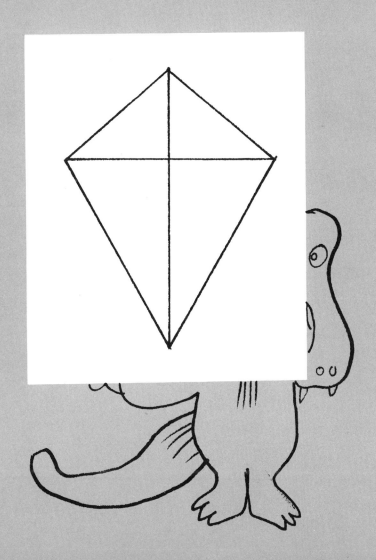

Besides line and point symmetries, there are still others. Look in a mirror. Your face and the face you see in the mirror balance on each side of the mirror. So do your arms and feet. Every part of you that you see in the mirror balances a part of the real you.

Now move your hand. The hand in the mirror also moves. No matter where you move your hand, it will be as far in front of the mirror as your mirror hand seems to be behind the mirror. Your hand and the mirror hand have the same shape and size. They balance on each side of the mirror.

They do not balance on each side of a line, or on each side of a point. The mirror is not a line; nor is it a point. It is a flat surface. We describe a flat surface as a plane. The balance between you and your mirror image is called PLANE SYMMETRY.

The two sides of this house are alike.

The house has plane symmetry. Where is its plane of symmetry?

In this picture the plane of symmetry is the surface of the water.

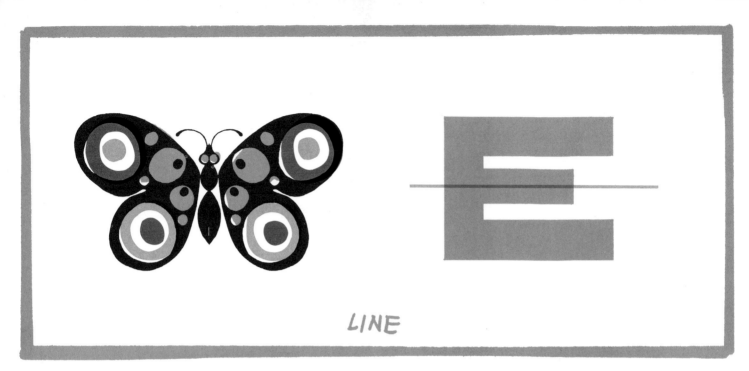

LINE

Now you know something about line symmetry, point symmetry, and plane symmetry. There are still other kinds of symmetry. Perhaps some day you will get to know them, too.

POINT

PLANE

ABOUT THE AUTHORS

What Is Symmetry? is the first book on which Mr. and Mrs. Sitomer have collaborated. Harry Sitomer was born in Russia and was educated in New York City. He has taught mathematics in both high school and college and is the coauthor of several mathematics textbooks. *What Is Symmetry?* reflects Mr. Sitomer's interest and active participation in the current changes in school mathematics.

Mindel Sitomer was born and educated in New York City. She studied biology in college, and says that when her own children were small she learned that young people easily understand and enjoy hearing about major scientific concepts. That is one of the reasons she enjoyed working with her husband to present this information about symmetry to young readers.

The Sitomers now live in Huntington, New York. They have two children and seven grandchildren.

ABOUT THE ILLUSTRATOR

Ed Emberley is usually busy writing and illustrating, but he does find time to pursue the strong family interest in all kinds of craft work. In fact, a new room is being added to their seventeenth-century home to accommodate the Emberley kiln.

In order to get away from the workbench occasionally, Mr. Emberley and his family go sailing and cross-country skiing.

Ed Emberley received a B.F.A. degree in illustration from the Massachusetts School of Art in Boston. He lives in Ipswich, Massachusetts.